The One-eyed Zoff

Written & Illustrated
by Amanda Graham

There was only one thing
that scared Ben Spring.

It wasn't the Ten-horned Trink
that lived under the sink,

or the Nine-toothed Grond
that lived in the pond,

or the Eight-eared Rable
that lived under the table,

or the Seven-tongued Sleezer
that lived in the freezer,

or the Six-handed Spled
that lived in the shed,

or the Five-winged Flarden
that lived in the garden,

or the Four-footed Vath
that lived in the bath,

or the Three-headed Slouch
that lived under the couch,

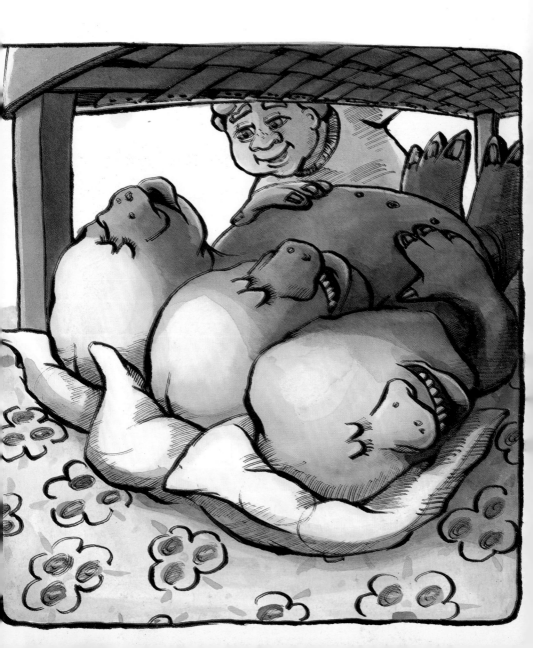

or the Two-nosed Smeller
that lived in the cellar.
The only thing that scared
Ben Spring

was the One-eyed Zoff
of Count von Droff.

But if it got TOO scary,
this One-eyed Zoff,
Ben Spring could simply

turn it off.